Titanic Trail
Cobh (Queenstown)

Michael Martin

TITANIC TRAIL

Published by:
The Titanic Trail Ltd.
"Mellieha"
Carrignafoy,
Cobh, Co. Cork,
Ireland.

Registered Trade Mark

Tel: 353 21 4815211
Mobile. +87 276 7218
E-mail: info@titanic.ie
Website: www.titanic.ie
Audioboo: Titanic100

Photographs by Geraldine Martin

Copyright© Michael Martin 2011 *(first published 1998)*

ISBN 095 4011 201

All rights reserved. No part of this book may be copied, reproduced or transmitted in any form or by any means without the permission of the publisher.

Titanic Trail, preserving our past to enrich our future.

Printed in Ireland by Collins Print & Packaging Ltd., Cork

Cobh and the Titanic Trail

Cobh, formerly known as Queenstown is a harbour town that boasts centuries of seafaring and maritime tradition. The town was originally known as the Cove of Cork but changed its name to Queenstown after the visit of Queen Victoria in August 1849. Later, as a result of Irish Independence the town was renamed Cobh, a phonetic Irish word, pronounced as Cove.

The history of Cobh is entwined with great ships, majestic liners and adventurous tales of the sea. It was a major centre of embarkation for Irish emigrants including those one hundred and twenty three passengers who boarded RMS Titanic at the mouth of the Harbour on the 11th April 1912. It was to be Titanic's last port of call. Having weighted anchor for the last time the ship sailed westward to the tragic encounter with an iceberg in the cold waters of the North Atlantic. Over 1500 people were lost and of the 123 who had boarded at Cobh or Queenstown as it was known then; only 44 survived.

The Titanic Trail guided walking tour of Cobh and this booklet explore the many connections with the ship and buildings, piers and sites associated with events of 1912. Additional military, maritime and emigrant heritage is also explored. Cobh today remains architecturally the same as it was a century ago and when a visitor walks along its streets they are walking in the same physical streetscape that the Titanic passengers did.

Michael Martin

About the Author

Michael Martin was born in Dublin in 1958. His career in the Irish Naval Service spanned 23 years and included a tour of duty with the United Nations in South Lebanon. Michael's interest in the Titanic goes back a number of years and is one of a wide range of interests which he pursues with vigour. He has delivered presentations and lectures on Cobh in the US, the UK and Australia. In the early 1990s Michael was instrumental in establishing the constitutional right of members of the armed forces to form Representative Bodies in Ireland. This had necessitated taking the Government and the people of Ireland to the High Court. His success there required the enactment of new legislation by the national parliament. He became Ireland's first General Secretary of the Permanent Defence Force Other Ranks Representative Association. Michael returned to College as a mature student in 2004 and graduated from University College Cork with a First Class Honours Degree in History in 2007. He then undertook a PhD at UCC and conducted part of his doctoral research as a visiting Scholar at the University of California Berkeley. He was conferred with his Doctorate at University College Cork in 2011. He has lived in Cobh with his wife Geraldine and two sons, Ken and Gary for many years.

Acknowledgments

Mr. Ted Walker for recreation of his painting "Into The Night"
The Wilson Collection
Cork County Library
Cobh UDC
The author would like to acknowledge all of those too numerous to list who provided support, advice and inspiration for the writing of this book.

Titanic Trail Project

The idea for the original Titanic Trail Project was the brainchild of the author while serving as Chairman of Cobh Tourism. The intention was to provide a booklet that facilitated visitors undertaking their own informed walking tour of Cobh that would be augmented by Titanic Trail plaques marking points of interest. The Cobh and Harbour Chamber of Commerce underwrote the initial cost of setting up the project. It was grant aided by East Cork Area Development and generously supported by the business people of Cobh.

Titanic, an Eternal Legacy

The brief visit of RMS Titanic to Cork Harbour on 11th April 1912 was the beginning of the final stages of one of the world's most enduring maritime legacies. Although on the day in question, the visit of the great liner was a rather ordinary affair. Thousands of ships before and after Titanic made such a stop though few elicited the world attention that its sinking provoked. A century on, the debate, conjecture and speculation about the ship and the tragedy continues. Enthusiasts still marvel at the length, breadth, style and appearance of Titanic despite untold advances in all these areas in the intervening years. Scientists still seek answers from her submerged hull despite the incredible depth at which she lies. They often emerge from years of research with more questions than answers. Speculation still abounds about the cause of the tragedy, the wisdom of the captain, the methodology of the lifesaving measures and the propensity for higher class passengers to have had a better chance of survival than those in steerage. In many respects the Titanic tragedy prompted the re-examination of values, standards and deeply held convictions about class and station. The passengers and crew of the ship were a microcosm of society generally. The same attitudes, fears and perspectives of the various classes in society were reflected on board. The catastrophic loss of life touched them all. In Cobh today the very buildings that passengers left from, the accommodations where they slept, the railroad that they came on are all still here. However routine the visit of the ship may have been, its legacy has remained and can be enjoyed in the veritable living museum that is the town today.

 # DEEPWATER QUAY & RAILWAY STATION

The rail link between Cork and Cobh (known then as Queenstown) was constructed in in the early 1860s to facilitate the increasing emigrant, mail and business traffic to and from the harbour as it grew into one of Europe's most important transatlantic ports. The design was reputedly overseen by the noted Victorian engineer, Brunel. The short journey is a delightful one, crossing islands and estuaries as it makes its way to Cobh on Great Island. As economic and social conditions improved and deteriorated the rate of emigration ebbed and flowed and it is thought that over two and a half million emigrants embarked from Cobh through the 19th and 20th centuries. The iconic sculpture of Annie Moore by Jeananne Ryanhart stands in front the railway station today, she was the first person to be processed through Ellis Island on the day of its official opening on 1st January 1892.

The Deepwater Quay beside the railway station was developed in 1882 and was utilised as a place of passenger disembarkation, customs, mail pick-up and dispatch point. The two tenders, PS Ireland and PS America berthed briefly here with Titanic passengers having left the White Star Line terminal building on 11th April 1912. Mail for and from the ill fated ship was exchanged here for movement by rail.

Development of the quay has continued so that today some of the largest cruise liners in the world can berth safely alongside the historical town of Cobh.

TITANIC TRAIL 2 — OLD YACHT CLUB

Currently housing the Sirius Arts Centre, the Cobh and Harbour Chamber of Commerce and Cobh's Tourist Information Office, the Old Yacht Club was built in 1854. It was the headquarters of the Royal Cork Yacht Club from that date until 1965. The forerunner of the RCYC was the 'Water Club' which was established on nearby Haulbowline Island in 1720 by two military officers who sought the permission of their King create a club that would 'sail for leisure'. Being the first club of its kind, it remains today the oldest Yacht Club in the world, having moved across the harbour to a new location in 1965.

The name Sirius derives from the first steamer to cross the Atlantic without the use of a sail. It left from Passage West which is a short distance upriver from Cobh and arrived to great acclaim in New York on 22nd April 1838.

COMMODORE HOTEL FORMERLY QUEEN'S HOTEL

This Hotel, known today as the Commodore was built in 1855 and named the Queen's Hotel in honour of the visit of Queen Victoria to Cobh in 1849. It was used to assist in accommodating the survivors from the Lusitania in 1915 while under the ownership of the German family Humbert. In the early 1920s the hotel was renamed the States Hotel.

It opened and closed several times up until 1939 when it was refurbished, renamed the Commodore only to close down again at the start of the second world war. The Commodore reopened in 1947. It is operated today by the O'Shea family and contains a wonderful gallery of photographs of Jack Doyle, Cobh's most famous son.

TITANIC TRAIL 4 — LUSITANIA PEACE MEMORIAL

During the First World War in May 1915, the Cunard passenger liner RMS Lusitania was struck by a torpedo fired from a German submarine. The incident occurred off the Old Head of Kinsale and Southwest of the entrance of Cork Harbour. It was reported that the ship sank in only 18 minutes.

1,198 passengers and crew died as a result. Almost immediately after the rescue operation began, it was ordered that all survivors and victims be brought into Cobh (then known as Queenstown). In the days and weeks that followed local townspeople were confronted daily by the trauma and tragedy of loss experienced by those bereaved. The Lusitania Peace Memorial commemorates those who were lost and pays tribute to the local fishermen and others who made repeated journeys out and back to the site of the sinking ship in an effort to save as many as possible. Over 760 people were rescued.

At the northern end of Casement Square stands the arched building housing the Cobh Library. This was a municipal building at the time of the Lusitania sinking and was used as a temporary morgue. It was originally constructed as a Market House in 1806 by Mr. Smith Barry of Fota House, whose family crest can be seen on the pediment.

TITANIC MEMORIAL *Pearse Square*

This memorial stands on the corner of Pearse Square in the centre of town. It was unveiled in July 1998 in the presence of Milvina Dean a survivor of the Titanic. It commemorates all those lost on the ship. The Bronze relief on the monument depicts passengers on board the tender PS America being brought out to the great ship itself. The image of the lady with a number of children on the relief is that of Mrs Margaret Rice. The loss of Mrs Rice and her 5 children represents the largest single family loss of any Irish families aboard.

When the remains of Margaret Rice was found in the water she had a bottle of pills in her coat pocket. The pharmacist whose address was on the label was able to assist in the confirmation of her identity by reference to his prescription of the tablets to her on the 9th of April, just 2 days before her embarkation aboard Titanic.

TITANIC TRAIL — 6 — WHITE STAR LINE OFFICE

This building was erected in the 1830s. In 1912 it housed the White Star Line Office under the agency of James Scott and Company. Passengers for all White Star Line ships including those for Titanic checked in here. Cabin class passengers were accommodated on the first floor of the building overlooking the harbour while third class queued in line down the ramp at the side of the building.

The pier at the rear of the building is still visible today. It was from this pier that passengers for Titanic stepped off dry land for the last time before boarding the tenders that would take them to the great ship lying anchored off Roche's Point. Those left ashore would have walked along and up the town to get a last glimpse of their relatives on their way out the harbour. Of the 123 passengers who embarked Titanic from here only 44 survived.

TITANIC TRAIL 6A OLD SOLDIERS' HOME

This building is known as the Old Soldiers' Home. It has served as a premises of the Royal Cork Yacht Club, a Post Office, a Soldiers' Home and Sailors' Rest and probably most importantly as an Emigrants' Home. In the 1880s Charlotte Grace O'Brien conducted a campaign to try and improve the stark conditions that emigrants had to endure in their efforts to get to the New World. She set up the Emigrants' Home to provide clean healthy conditions where emigrants could stay without fear of being set upon by greedy opportunists who would demand exorbitant rates for food and lodgings that were little more than gruel and squalor. Miss O'Brien was the daughter of W. Smith O'Brien, a well known Irish patriot who was transported to Van Diemen's Land following the failed uprising he led in County Tipperary in 1848.

TITANIC TRAIL 6B   WEST BEACH

12A West Beach pictured left was the home and business premises of Andrew William McIntosh in the mid 1800's. It is believed that Andrew William was a pilot who like many others combined the business of piloting ships into the Harbour with that of supplying them with goods and provisions for their outward journeys.

Later Andrew and a number of his friends salvaged a ship that had been abandoned off Cobh. The considerable fortune he made enabled him to travel the world in an entrepreneurial spirit.

During the Ballarat Gold Rush of Australia he found a large gold nugget. Records show that he then proceeded to Japan and was listed as a hotelier. He is reputed to have been the first Westerner to import bicycles into Japan where he stayed for two years. Later he had a gold watch made from the nugget he had found which is still a family heirloom in the possession of his great grandson Derek McIntosh. Derek occasionally comes to Cobh where he can visit the grave of Andrew William who is interred in Clonmel Cemetery locally known as the Old Church Cemetery.

TITANIC TRAIL 7 CUNARD LINE OFFICE

This building which is currently occupied by the Trustee Savings Bank was formerly the Cunard Line Office.

At the rear of the building next door was the Cunard Pier, little remains of it today. It was at this pier that the first victims of the Lusitania were brought ashore. Outside this building huge numbers of sympathisers gathered and witnessed first hand the distress of survivors who had experienced great tragedy. In later years the Cunard and White Star lines merged and became the Cunard White Star Line. Eventually they dropped White Star and became the Cunard Line. Although the office is long gone Cunard Liners still come to Cobh.

Lynch's Quay and former Harbour Commissioners Office

Lynch's Quay is the oldest named quay in Cobh and is often referred to as the Ballast Quay. This name originates from the practice of ships in days gone by.

They unloaded their precious cargoes here which emptied their holds. It was then necessary to fill the same holds again with various materials including boulders to give stability and weight to the vessel for her outward journey in search of more trade and cargo. The building was once the local office of the Cork Harbour Commissioners. It was built in 1874 against much opposition because it impeded the view of residents and traders of East Beach. Two memorials stand outside the building today. One commemorates all Irishmen who were lost at sea in the service of the State over the years. The other is a memorial to the men who lost their lives in a tragic shipping incident in the Harbour in 1942.

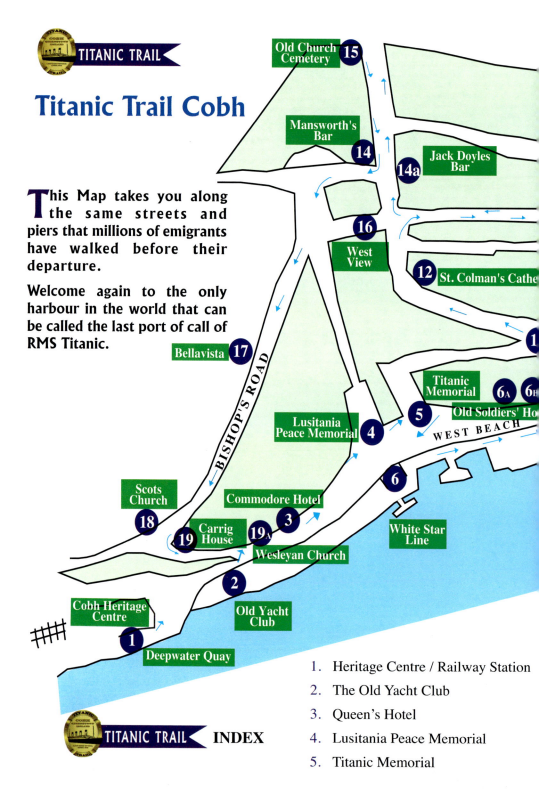

Information Plaques

Where necessary Sites are identified by a Bronze Titanic Trail Information Plaque in or near the place of interest.

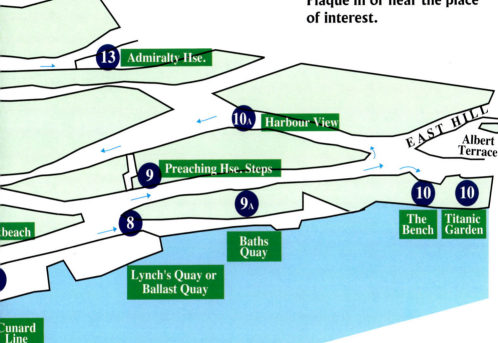

6. White Star Line
6A. The Old Soldiers' Home
6B. Westbeach
7. Cunard Line
8. Lynch's Quay / Ballast Quay
9. Preaching House Steps
9A. Baths Quay
10. The Bench
10. Titanic Garden
10A. Harbour View
11. Cathedral Walk
12. St. Colman's Cathedral
13. Admiralty Hse.
14. Mansworth's Bar
14A Jack Doyle's Bar
15. The Old Cemetery
16. West View
17. Bellavista
18. Scots Church
19. Carrig House
19A. Wesleyan Church

TITANIC TRAIL 9 & 9A PREACHING HOUSE STEPS

These steps were used by people who made their way to the first Methodist preaching house opened in 1810 which was located on the terraces above, hence the name, the "Preaching House Steps". The Quay which can be seen from the opposite side of the street was formerly known as Inmans Quay. This later became Baths Quay which refers to Public Bathing Baths that were built in 1878. In later years these baths were reportedly used as an emigrant "cleansing station" for intending emigrants to America. During the first World War an American Naval Men's Club was erected on this quay for the recreation and leisure of US service personnel stationed in the Harbour during World War I.

TITANIC TRAIL 10 THE BENCH

The Bench is a well known and popular meeting place overlooking the entrance of Cork Harbour. It got its name from the fact that sailors, traders and townspeople have met there for generations and conversed on all matters of greater and lesser importance. The perceived collective wisdom was so great it was likened to that which one would receive from a judge on the King's Bench.

Elderly sailors and those with an interest in all things maritime gathered here over the years. Conversations, recalling earlier experiences of lifetimes at sea, were interrupted only to comment on a passing ship or craft. Walking further to the east of the Bench the Titanic Commemorative Garden contains a glass wall through which can be seen the entrance to the harbour where RMS Titanic lay at anchor on the 11th of April 1912. The Pilot for the Titanic that day was a Mr. John Cotter who lived nearby. The names of the 123 people who boarded Titanic from Cobh are etched on the commemorative glass which was erected by Cobh Town Council and a number of community groups following suggestions made by the author Michael Martin. He had been greatly impressed by a similar glass etched wall naming famine victims on Grosse Ille in Canada.

Pilot John Cotter

TITANIC TRAIL 10A HARBOUR VIEW

Walking up along Harbour View from the Bench to the Cathedral provides a panoramic view of the harbour. Its centre is dominated by Spike Island. The island was the site of a monastic settlement in the seventh century. Later the British Military placed cannons there to deter the Spanish Armada. The military fortifications on the island were upgraded in the early 1790's and adopted for use in 1847 as a holding prison for convicts who were bound for 'transportation' to Australia. Many of these so called convicts had in fact been criminalised by their hunger, finding themselves having to steal food or poach on others property in a desperate attempt to feed their families. Those lucky enough to survive the harsh conditions were subjected to torturous voyages of eight months or more to Australia and Tasmania. During these protracted periods the convicts were kept in chains at all times. John Mitchel, a famous Irish patriot, writer and poet was held on Spike Island in 1848 before being transported to Van Diemans Land.

TITANIC TRAIL 11 CATHEDRAL WALK

This area would have been visited by departing emigrants' families who climbed the steep streets in order to gain a better vantage point from which to see the departing ships and wave goodbye to their loved ones.

TITANIC TRAIL — 12 — ST. COLMAN'S CATHEDRAL

St Colman's Cathedral is the most dominant architectural feature of lower Cork harbour. It enshrines the tradition of thirteen centuries of the Diocese of Cloyne. The Cathedral is named after St Colman (522-604) who is the patron saint of the Diocese.

Construction began in 1868 and although it took over fifty years to complete, mass was first celebrated there in 1879. The style of the church is French neo-gothic with the predominant stone of the exterior comprising of Dalkey blue granite with Mallow limestone dressings.

The architectural team were Ashlin, Coleman and Pugin the younger. The interior boasts magnificent examples of the very best of Irish, British, French and Italian craftsmanship of the period in its stain-glass windows, marble carvings, stonework and carpentry. The cost of the project over its fifty years of construction amounted to £235,000 pounds of £90,000 was collected in the locality. The remaining £145,000 was collected throughout the Diocese and from benefactors and emigrants in Australia, America and elsewhere. It has come to be known by some as the emigrants cathedral reflecting the huge number of Irish emigrants who worshipped here before embarking on their life changing journeys to a new life in a new country elsewhere.

Following the sinking of RMS Titanic, the church conducted a requiem mass in the knowledge that just a few days earlier, many of those who had perished had come there to get their last mass and Holy Communion before their fateful journey. As those Titanic passenger had left Cobh, the spire on the cathedral was not yet complete. It was finished in 1915 and soon after the Republic of Ireland's only carillon was installed. Originally consisting of 42 bells, five were added in 1958 and another two brought the total to forty nine! This makes the carillon of St Colman's the largest in Ireland and Great Britain. The largest bell weighs 3.6 tonnes and has a base diameter of 5 feet or 1.6 metres, it is known as St Colman. The smallest bell is just one kilogram! It is an instrument that is regularly played for religious events but also for recitals on Sunday afternoons from May to September during which classical and even popular tunes can be heard. The cathedral is an important feature of Cobh's ecclesiastical heritage and is inextricably linked with its emigrant history too.

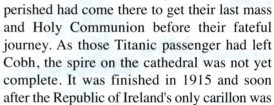

Admiralty House

Although this building dates to 1886 it was the second such house built for the Admiralty. The first which was sited nearby was erected in 1765.

This was the residence of the Naval Commander in Chief of Queenstown. The house commanded a watchful eye on the harbour and could signal by way of flags to naval ships anchored there.

Following Independence in 1922 the House was set alight by Republican Forces. It was later purchased by the Catholic church who refurbished it and set it up as a Noviciate for the Sisters of Mercy. In 1993 the house was bought by the Benedictine Sisters who operate it today as a contemplative monastery.

TITANIC TRAIL 14 — Mansworth's Bar

This establishment has the longest tradition of family ownership in the Town. The Mansworth family have owned the pub since 1895. They undoubtedly served ale to many of the relatives and friends of the emigrants who left Cobh in their millions.

14a — Jack Doyles Bar

This warm traditional Irish Bar is dedicated to Cobh's most famous son, Jack Doyle. It was re-opened by Pat and Ruth Kidney in 2002. They invited Jack's nephew Chris to launch the opening which he did with the grace and charm of his uncle.

All visitors on the Titanic Trail guided walking tour are offered a complimentary glass of Guinness here during their walk.

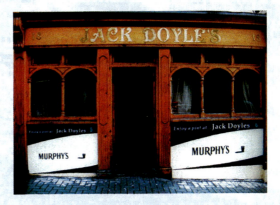

THE OLD CHURCH CEMETERY

Clonmel cemetery (just under 1 mile from the town centre) has been in use as a place of worship and burial going back to Celtic times. The earliest headstone date that is still visible is that of Stephen Towes 1698. There are a number of mass graves there however.

The Cemetery is where the remains of 170 victims of the Lusitania are interred in three mass graves and twenty four individual plots. Forty five of them remain unidentified. In 1915 the whole town witnessed the heartbreaking processions of multiple funerals making their way from the town to here. It is known locally as the Old Church Cemetery. The remains of many famous people are buried here.

Among them Dr. James Roche Verling, a native of Cobh, who was personal physician to Napoleon Bonaparte, Jack Doyle famous as the "Gorgeous Gael," actor, boxer and hero to thousands of Irish men an women, and poet Charles Wolfe. The cemetery is also a resting place for many Naval and Military personnel killed in World War conflicts. Personnel who fought in Ireland's War of Independance on opposite sides also lie here equal in death.

TITANIC TRAIL 16 WEST VIEW

Looking out from this vantage point one can again see the anchorage where the Titanic lay in wait for her mail and passengers. The twenty three multicoloured houses which were built in the mid 1800s are known as the "pack of cards" locally and were built on twenty three different levels. The small passageway just over the wall is affectionately known as the Khyber Pass.

TITANIC TRAIL 17 BELLAVISTA

This house was built in 1845 and has had a colourful history attached to it from its earliest day. Dr. James Roche Verling, a native of Cobh lived here for a number of years. He was personal physician to Napoleon Bonaparte on St. Helena from 1818 to 1820. The eminent doctor died in 1858 and is buried in the Old Church Cemetery.

The Carbery family who were renowned for their relief work during the Great Irish Famine bought the house and lived here until 1914. Having been purchased by Bishop Robert Browne the house was officially opened in November 1916 and blessed as the Sacred Heart Noviciate. Father Browne, a nephew of the Bishop, had been a first class passenger on the Titanic from Southampton to Queenstown. He frequently visited this house. He gave lectures on the Titanic here and displayed his prolific collection of photographs of the ship. Many of these photographs were used by the international media following the tragedy. Father Browne also celebrated Mass here. His pictures were the only surviving photographic record of people on the ill fated ship at sea. They have been used over the years by film makers, publishers and authors, and have enriched the collective memories of all.

Scots Church

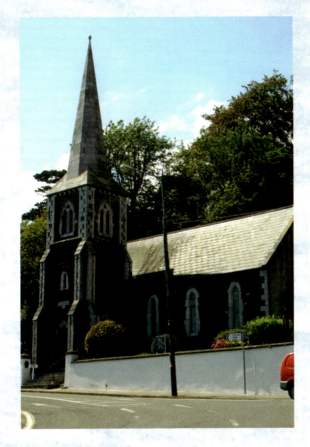

Built in 1854 to meet the needs of the Presbyterian community of Cobh, this church was closed in 1969, due to a dwindling congregation. Since 1973 it has operated as Cobh Museum. The main interior features of the church remain, including the pulpit, lectern, harmonium and original bible. The displays reflect the social, cultural and maritime history of the town.

Carrig House

This house was built in 1850 by a Mr. John Atkins who was a wealthy merchant at that time. It changed hands in the 1890s and then several times again until it was bought for use as the American Consulate in the 1920s. It remained so until 1933 after which it was bought by the Department of Education. It was used as a vocational school and an Irish Language school in recent years. In 2003 the offices of Cobh Town Council moved from their former location near Lynch's quay to Carrig House. The new Council Chamber hosts the formal meeting of the Council every month. It is also the venue for Civic Receptions and awards afforded to visiting dignitaries and citizens of note.

DON'T FORGET DAILY GUIDED WALKING TOURS FROM THE COMMODORE HOTEL, 11AM EVERY DAY *(Book at www.titanic.ie)*

Titanic Trail
Guided Heritage Activities

ORGANISED HISTORICAL SEMINARS, GROUP TOURS & SCHOOL OUTINGS.

FOR A RANGE OF QUALITY CULTURAL ACTIVITIES
CONTACT MICHAEL MARTIN,
MELLIEHA, CARRIGNAFOY, COBH, CO. CORK, IRELAND.

Tel: 353 21 4815211   Mobile: +353 87 276 7218
website: www.titanic.ie   E-mail: info@titanic.ie

Rev. John Wesley

The Rev. John Wesley founder of the Methodist Church visited Cobh in the 1760's. He was reputed to have denounced Cobh as a "Godless place" and went on to describe it's citizens as a "Sinful sink of sinners".

Groups of preachers were soon organised to bring the ways of God to town. The street preaching was upgraded in 1810 when a preaching house was opened on the terraces overlooking the water on Harbour View. In 1873 however the preaching house was vacated when the magnificent Wesleyan Church pictured left was built. The interior today is beautifully finished in stylish decor however it is unlikely that the Rev. John Wesley would be impressed! The tasteful decoration, the relaxing ambience is that of a bar. Pillars Bar one of Cobh's finest, serving beer and playing music, but would not be quite what the Reverend had in mind.

Titanic Trail Plaques

The Titanic Trail plaques have been generously sponsored by the following:

Deepwater Quay, Railway Station .... Cobh Heritage Centre

Queen's Hotel .... Patrick O'Shea, Commodore Hotel

Lusitania Peace Memorial .... Tom and Imelda Kelly, Rotunda Bar

White Star Line Office .... Vince Keaney

Cunard Line Office .... Trustee Savings Bank

Ballast Quay, Town Hall .... Robbie and Jackie Watson, The Well House

St. Colman's Cathedral .... Bishop of Cloyne

Admiralty House............. Noreen Hickey, Mount View, Guest Accommodation

Mansworth's Bar .... John Mansworth

Old Cemetery .... Jim Murphy, Ticknock Service Station

West View .... Ray and Maura Keating, Centra Supermarket

Bellavista, Guest Accommodation .... Peggy O'Rourke

Preaching House Steps............................. Liz Hannon, English Auctioneers

The Bench......................... Martha Hurley, Highland, Guest Accommodation